MEET THE DINOSAURS!: WHEN REPTILES RULED

MEET THE MEAT-EATING DINOSAURS

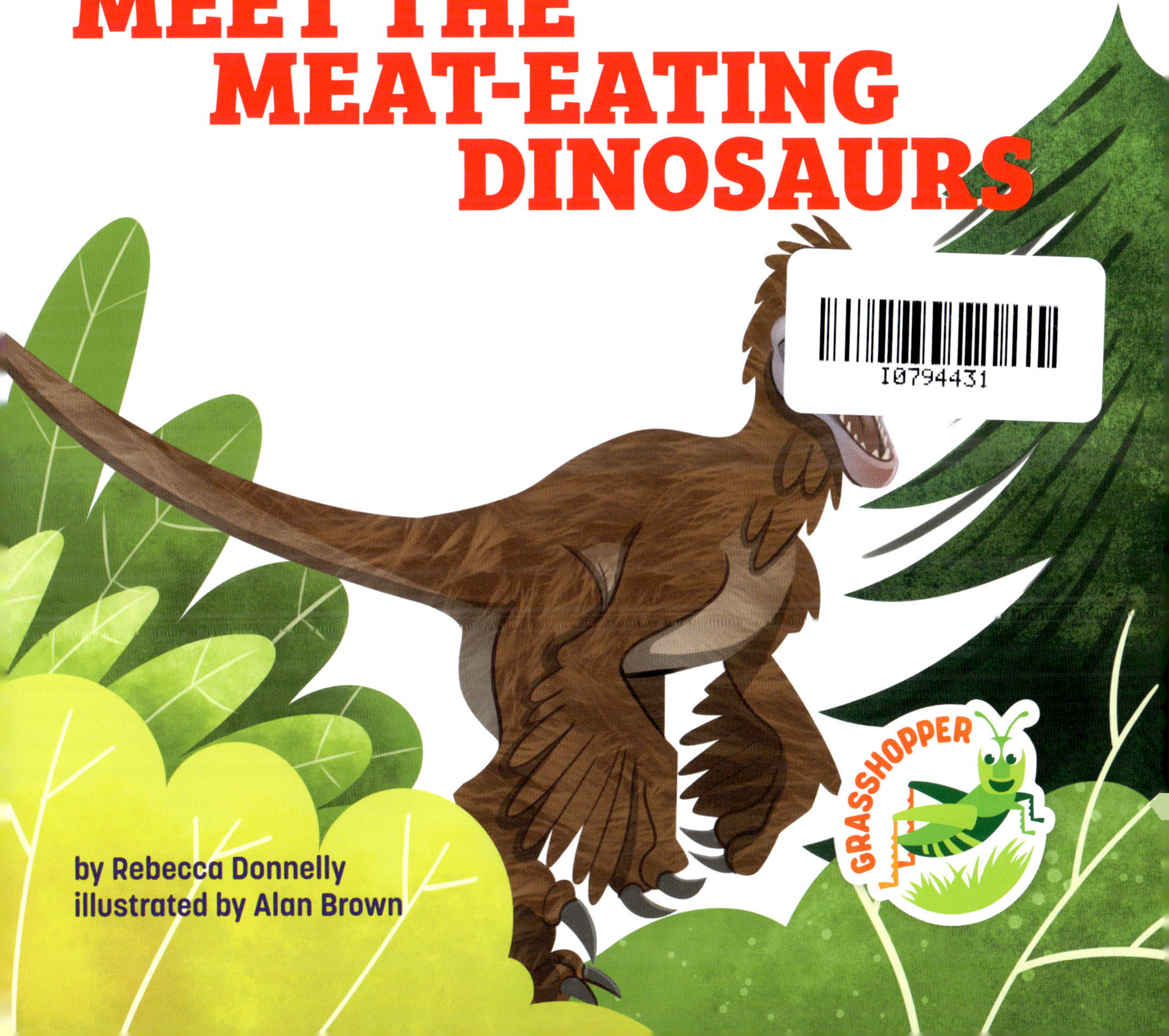

by Rebecca Donnelly
illustrated by Alan Brown

GRASSHOPPER

Tools for Parents & Teachers

Grasshopper Books enhance imagination and introduce the earliest readers to fiction with fun storylines and illustrations. The easy-to-read text supports early reading experiences with repetitive sentence patterns and sight words.

Before Reading

- Discuss the cover illustration. What do they see?
- Look at the glossary together. Discuss the words.

Read the Book

- Read the book to the child, or have him or her read independently.
- "Walk" through the book and look at the illustrations. What is happening in the story?

After Reading

- Prompt the child to think more. Ask: There were many meat-eating dinosaurs. What carnivores do you know of that live today? Do you know what animals they hunt and eat?

Grasshopper Books are published by Jump!
5357 Penn Avenue South
Minneapolis, MN 55419
www.jumplibrary.com

Library of Congress Cataloging-in-Publication Data

Names: Donnelly, Rebecca, author.
Brown, Alan, illustrator.
Title: Meet the meat-eating dinosaurs / Rebecca Donnelly; illustrated by Alan Brown.
Description: Minneapolis, MN: Jump!, Inc., [2022]
Series: Meet the dinosaurs!: when reptiles ruled
Includes index.
Audience: Ages 7-10
Identifiers: LCCN 2021037967 (print)
LCCN 2021037968 (ebook)
ISBN 9781636906119 (hardcover)
ISBN 9781636906126 (paperback)
ISBN 9781636906133 (ebook)
Subjects: LCSH: Dinosaurs–Food–Juvenile literature.
Classification: LCC QE861.5 .D6845 2022 (print)
LCC QE861.5 (ebook)
DDC 567.9/37–dc23
LC record available at https://lccn.loc.gov/2021037967
LC ebook record available at https://lccn.loc.gov/2021037968

Editor: Eliza Leahy
Direction and Layout: Anna Peterson
Illustrator: Alan Brown

Printed in the United States of America at Corporate Graphics in North Mankato, Minnesota.

Table of Contents

Fast and Strong

I'm Victor the Velociraptor. I may be a small dinosaur, but I'm speedy! Carnivores like me have to be fast to catch prey.

We're all great hunters, but a lot of us are scavengers, too! We'll eat any kind of meat, even if it's already dead. Let's meet some other meat-eating dinosaurs!

Hi, I'm Cici the Coelophysis. I'm fast, like Victor. I have sharp, curved claws to catch prey. My favorite foods are small reptiles and mammals.

claw
reptile

I’m Ursula the Utahraptor. I’m much bigger and scarier than Victor and Cici!

I hunt with other Utahraptors. We use our long claws to slash prey. Then we bite with our sharp teeth!

Lots of dinosaurs hunt on land, but I hunt in the water! I'm Sami the Spinosaurus. I snatch fish with my long jaws. I'm the biggest carnivorous dinosaur!

And I'm one of the smallest!
I'm Mei the Microraptor.
I hunt in the air. I glide from
trees to snag my prey!

I'm Haley the Hesperonychus. I'm small, but my razor-sharp claws and teeth make me a deadly hunter. I catch tiny mammals, insects, and other small animals.

I'm Carter the Carnotaurus. We all have tiny arms. But we're the only two-legged meat-eaters with horns. We use them to fight. Thick scales on our backs protect us. *Wham!*

horn
scale

I'm Dylan the Dilophosaurus. See these two crests on my head? They help me attract a mate.

I'm a fierce hunter, too. I have strong arms and long, sharp claws. I chomp my prey with my powerful jaws. *Snap!*

Al the Allosaurus here! These other carnivores think they're tough, but can they take down a Stegosaurus?

My legs are so powerful, I can run 21 miles (34 kilometers) per hour! I chase my prey. Then I slice it with my sharp teeth.

I'm Tracy the Tyrannosaurus rex, queen of the carnivores! I'm 40 feet (12 meters) long and 13 feet (4.0 m) tall. My biggest teeth are 12 inches (30 centimeters) long.

All of us dinosaurs are extinct now, though. No more meat-eating for me!

Timeline

Dinosaurs lived millions of years ago. Take a look at when the dinosaurs in this book lived!

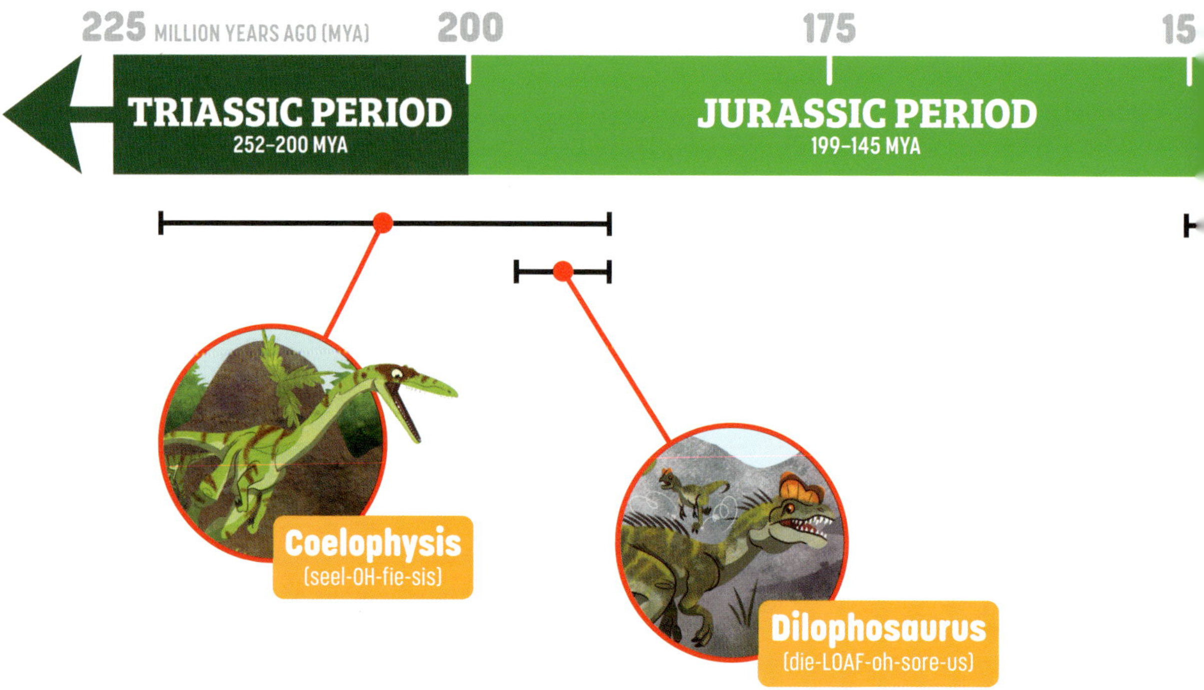

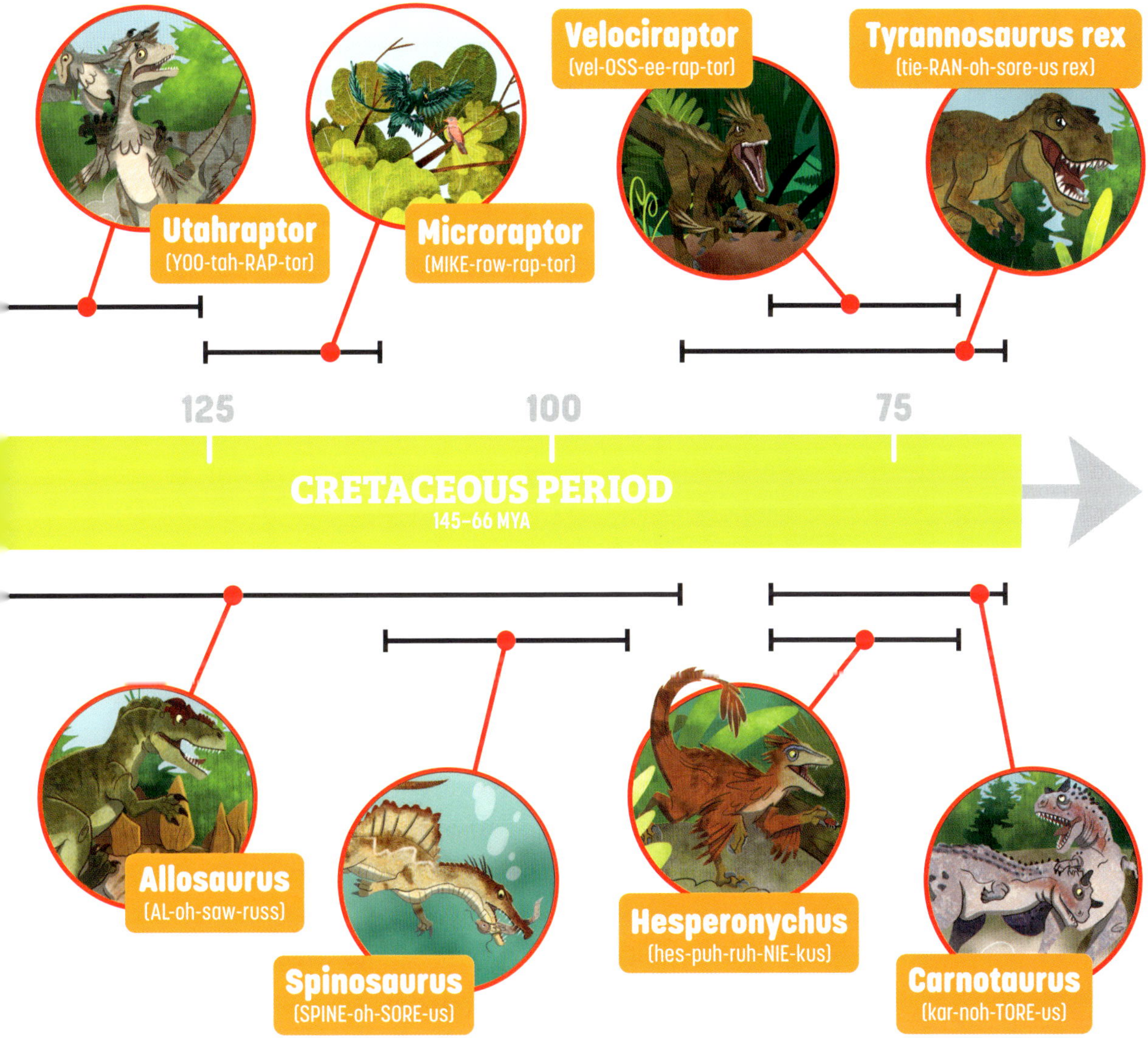
Velociraptor
(vel-OSS-ee-rap-tor)
Tyrannosaurus rex
(tie-RAN-oh-sore-us rex)
Utahraptor
(YOO-tah-RAP-tor)
Microraptor
(MIKE-row-rap-tor)
125
100
75
CRETACEOUS PERIOD
145–66 MYA
Allosaurus
(AL-oh-saw-russ)
Spinosaurus
(SPINE-oh-SORE-us)
Hesperonychus
(hes-puh-ruh-NIE-kus)
Carnotaurus
(kar-noh-TORE-us)

Glossary

attract: To get something's interest.

carnivores: Animals that eat meat.

extinct: No longer found alive and known about only through fossils or history.

mammals: Warm-blooded animals that give birth to live young.

mate: One member of a breeding pair of animals.

prey: Animals that are hunted by other animals for food.

reptiles: Cold-blooded animals that crawl across the ground or creep on short legs.

scavengers: Animals that feed on dead or decaying material.

Index

To Learn More

FACT SURFER

Finding more information is as easy as 1, 2, 3.

1. Go to www.factsurfer.com
2. Enter "**meetthemeat-eatingdinosaurs**" into the search box.
3. Choose your book to see a list of websites.